NINE SHORT PIECES

from Three Centuries

Arranged for oboe and piano by

Roy Thackray

Contents

Oxford University Press

12-95

NINE SHORT PIECES
from Three Centuries
THREE 17th CENTURY PIECES

I. SARABAND
(from the 1st Quartet for Viols)

M. LOCKE
(1622 - 1677)

II. PRELUDE and GAVOTTA
(from the Concerti Grossi)

A. CORELLI
(1653 - 1713)

4

III. AIR
(from the Harpsichord pieces)

H. PURCELL
(1659 - 1695)

THREE 18th CENTURY PIECES

I. SICILIANO
(from the Oratorio *'Susanna'*)

G. F. HANDEL
(1685 - 1759)

II. LARGO

(from the Concerto *'Winter'*, no.4 of *'The Four Seasons'*)

A. VIVALDI
(1675 - 1741)

'To spend quiet and happy days by the fire, while others are being drenched by the rain'.

NINE
SHORT
PIECES

from Three Centuries

Arranged for oboe and piano by
Roy Thackray

Oxford University Press

2

NINE SHORT PIECES
from Three Centuries
THREE 17th CENTURY PIECES

Oboe

I. SARABAND
(from the 1st Quartet for Viols)

M. LOCKE
(1622-1677)

II. PRELUDE and GAVOTTA
(from the Concerti Grossi)

A. CORELLI
(1653-1713)

III. AIR
(from the Harpsichord pieces)

H. PURCELL
(1659-1695)

THREE 18th CENTURY PIECES

I. SICILIANO
(from the Oratorio *'Susanna'*)

G. F. HANDEL
(1685-1759)

II. LARGO
(from the Concerto *'Winter'*, no.4 of *'The Four Seasons'*)

A. VIVALDI
(1675-1741)

'To spend quiet and happy days by the fire, while others are being drenched by the rain'

III. RIGAUDON
(from *Pièces de Clavecin,* Book 2)

J. Ph. RAMEAU
(1683-1764)

THREE 19th CENTURY PIECES

I. REVERIE

(from *'Album for the Young'*)

P. TCHAIKOVSKY Op. 39
(1840-1893)

II. INTERMEZZO

(from Organ Sonata No.4)

J. RHEINBERGER Op. 98
(1839-1901)

III. THE SONG OF THE ITALIAN SAILORS
(from *'Album for the Young'*)

R. SCHUMANN
(1810-1856)

Reproduced and printed by
Halstan & Co. Ltd., Amersham, Bucks., England

9

III. RIGAUDON

(from *Pièces de Clavecin*, Book 2)

J. Ph. RAMEAU
(1683 - 1764)

THREE 19th CENTURY PIECES

I. REVERIE

(from *'Album for the Young'*)

P. TCHAIKOVSKY Op. 39
(1840 - 1893)

Fine

D. C.

II. INTERMEZZO
(from Organ Sonata No. 4)

J. RHEINBERGER Op. 98
(1839 - 1901)

III. THE SONG OF THE ITALIAN SAILORS

(from *Album for the Young*)

R. SCHUMANN
(1810 - 1856)